WILD CHILD

ADVENTURE COOKING WITH KIDS
BY SARAH GLOVER

PHOTOGRAPHY BY
KAT PARKER

Prestel

Munich • London • New York

INTRO

I'LL NEVER FORGET THE FIRST TIME I CAUGHT A FISH.

Sure, twelve-year-old me wasn't crazy about gutting it, but the fact that we could source our own food in the wild—away from running water, a pantry, or fridge—awakened my creativity. It still does. We cooked the fresh fillets over coals and served them with spuds boiled in ocean water. Afterwards, we licked our fingers, the salt still tingling our taste buds. By nightfall, we had warm bellies and a hankering for adventure. It was the first time I'd cooked over a campfire and I was hooked.

Growing up in Australia, the woods were our backyard. I spent a lot of time exploring the wilderness with my brothers by my side. We were taught to love the outdoors; it was a place to be explored and embraced— somewhere we could be completely ourselves. It was the 80s, after all, and the world was our (hand-caught) oyster. Some of my fondest memories are from days spent camping in the bush or by the sea, with nothing but each other, a few fishing rods, and our imaginations to keep us occupied. Sticks made great swords. Treetops became make-believe castles. Mud was our paint, the earth was our canvas. With a child's eye, anything and everything (except homework) is an adventure.

These memories became the blueprint for my adult life—one that I've spent exploring the wilderness in all its forms. I've cooked on clifftops in Patagonia, foraged for wild mushrooms on Flinders Island off Tasmania, and searched for cockle on my favorite sandy beaches. Curiosity, the kind we have as kids, is at the core of everything I cook and create. My first book, *Wild: Adventure Cookbook*, is a love letter to the great outdoors. It's a lesson in learning to love the simplicity of food and a celebration of the beautiful produce at our fingertips. This book is a continuation of that spirit; daring, creative and inspiring.

Wild Child is about keeping your inner-child alive, embarking on new journeys with the next generation, and teaching little ones the importance of nature and imagination. It's meant to inspire parents and kids to make new memories, to be confident at any age, and to have fun outdoors, whether on a beach, by the bush, or in your own backyard.

I've always loved being around kids. When I was younger, I even wanted to be a teacher. I guess being the second eldest of eight kids made me a bit of a second mum. When I wasn't running around trying to keep up with my siblings, I was in the kitchen, working out how to amuse my family with fun, playful food. A lot of the ideas in this book—necklaces made of dried pasta, fish cooked on a string, and snags cooked in a bag—came from those precious hours spent in the kitchen with my brothers and sisters.

I designed each chapter in this book to bring outdoor experiences to life. Playhouse brings Peter Pan to life with recipes inspired by Neverland, including self-saucing chocolate pudding cooked in a coconut. Little Women invites mothers and daughters to claim the campsite as their own, while Sibella & the Pirates calls for a floating raft, ready for lobster rolls and sticky buns with billy jam with a buccaneering crew. Join Jax in the Kids' Camp where corn is popped in a can and black bean mud cakes are made in the mud. And finally, hang out with Arlo and his mates as they float up the river in Down to the Sea.

This book suits kids of all ages, from toddlers to teens and every age in between. It's also a heap of fun for adults, offering an excuse to take life less seriously and embrace a little dirt. The recipes in these pages are nourishing—and chock full of veggies in all kinds of unexpected places (Zucchini in popcorn form! Bright green spinach wraps!)—but I've left room for comfort food, too. Just try my oozing campfire caramel crêpes.

There's never been a better time to step out of your comfort zone. To say "See ya!" to the television screen and "Hello!" to the great outdoors. I'm a big believer that time in nature is medicine for modern-day life. Away from the creature comforts of home, there's a whole world to discover. Sometimes it's awesome not to have a whole spice drawer at your disposal—it forces you to think outside the box. Forgot the frying pan? Try cooking in coals. Ran out of salt? Use some ocean water in your pan. Try. Fail. Learn. Life's meant to be messy!

Kids these days don't have the same opportunities to get wild like we did. This is our chance to show them what it's like to live—and thrive—in nature. Use this book as your guide. Consider it your invitation to adventure with little tuckers in tow. Explore. Create. Inspire. And above all, don't be afraid to get a little sand in your food.

Sarah x

HOW TO USE THIS BOOK

THINK OF THIS BOOK AS YOUR GREAT OUTDOORS GAME PLAN.

It guides you through recipes primed for cooking in the woods—the bush, as we say in Australia, where I live—the beach, or your own backyard, and suits kids (and adults!) of all ages. With a little bit of practice and patience, you'll be roasting fresh-caught fish over the campfire in no time.

I encourage you to plan ahead when you're cooking with kids. The night before you set out, or over breakfast the day of, sit down with your gang and choose what kind of adventure you want to go on. Will it be cheesy breakfast toasties in the backyard or smashed spuds on a sandy beach? Engage your kids—choose something they really want to do—and make an experience out of it. When you have a plan, head to the local shops or markets, load up your basket with the necessary ingredients and equipment (see page 12), and then set off for the day.

When you're camping with kids, safety is a top priority. Start an open conversation about the nature of cooking with fire. It's not something to be afraid of—in fact, it's one of the most natural and primal ways to cook. That being said, campfire cooking calls for respect, care, and common sense. Encourage kids to ask questions, to tune into their senses, and to always check with a supervising adult before going anywhere near the flames.

If you're lighting a fire for the first time, start small. Here are some of my campfire non-negotiables:

Make sure the area around your fire is clear of any plant debris and make sure there aren't any overhanging branches nearby.

Create a barrier between your fire and your camping area to stop the spread. I like to use large rocks to surround the space or dig a hole in the sand if you're on a beach. You can also purchase a firepit from your local hardware store.

Monitor your fire and build it incrementally, so it's just big and hot enough to cook on, but still manageable.

Cook over coals—not a direct flame. Coals radiate a steady, strong heat that you can adjust by using more or less coals, and by cooking closer or further away from the direct heat. You'll get coals from your hardwood once it burns down, or you can use hardwood charcoal available at your local hardware store.

Avoid briquettes, as most are filled with nasty chemicals and aren't good for cooking.

Keep a water bucket and shovel on hand to extinguish the fire once you're done.

Remember that charcoal and gas barbecues are great, too, as are portable gas hot plates. Use whatever is most appropriate to the time and space you have, and that makes you feel comfortable and at ease while cooking.

Kids are inquisitive by nature. Showing them how to cook outdoors and over fire is a great way to teach them to respect the process, while also making beautiful memories together. Outline some general safety rules before you start cooking, keep an eye on your fire at all times, and last but not least, have fun!

HOW TO BUILD A FIRE

THIS IS A STEP-BY-STEP GUIDE THAT BUILDS YOUR FIRE GRADUALLY. PLEASE REFER TO IMAGES FOR REFERENCE.

1. Create your fire bed

Make sure the space surrounding your campfire is clear—nothing should hang over or around your fire bed. You should also create a barrier between your fire and camping area—try surrounding it with large rocks (think the size of a soccer ball or football), or digging a sand pit if you're by the beach.

2. Start with tinder

Create a small pile of tinder—I use pine cones, gum (eucalyptus) leaves, or dry bark and leaves. Don't use green or wet wood, which will smoke a lot and not catch fire. If you don't have any dry tinder, you can use newspaper. Carefully light a match and add it to the tinder until it starts to burn.

3. Time for kindling

Tinder burns quickly, so you'll need leaves with a bit more oomph to keep your fire going. Kindling includes dry twigs or branches and should be added to the top of your fire after the tinder is lit. It'll gradually catch fire from the burning tinder and continue to build your flame.

4. Add your fuel wood

Once your kindling has caught alight, carefully add your fuel wood. These logs are more substantial in size and will help increase the heat and size of your fire. Look for logs about the size of your forearm.

5. Let it burn

We want to cook over the coals, not direct heat so it's best to let your fire burn down for an hour or so, adding more fuel wood as necessary, until you have steady burning embers.

6. Choose your gear

Whether you're using a tripod, cooking stand, or a grate, now's the time to set up your equipment over the embers.

7. Let's cook!

Since you're cooking over coals, it'll take a bit of time to find the right temperature. To increase heat, add more fuel wood to the fire and let it burn down. You can also move your pots and pans closer to the radiant heat of the coals. To decrease heat, let the fire burn down further or move your pots and pans further away from the coals.

8. Pack it up

When you're finished with your fire, break it up with a shovel first, then toss a bucket of water over the top and cover it up with leftover soil.

YOUR KIT

I DESIGNED THESE RECIPES TO BE QUICK, EASY, AND TASTY. THEY'RE NOT OVERLY COMPLICATED AND DON'T REQUIRE UNUSUAL EQUIPMENT.

I want you to focus on connecting with the ingredients and having fun with your kids—not fussing over how to use a meat thermometer or mandoline in the wild. Avoid plastic and go for metal items with wooden handles wherever you can.

In addition to basics like a good sharp knife, a wooden spoon, a long set of tongs, and a cutting board (if you don't have room in your bag, use a log instead!), here are my camping essentials:

Large Pot or Billyboil: *Whether you're boiling spuds or making a caramel sauce, a large pot is an all-round camping essential. I prefer one with a handle, so it can hang over the fire, doubling as a pot and a billyboil (a tall, narrow camping pot).*

Frying Pan: *Choose a light yet durable frying pan that measures around 12 inches (30 cm) in diameter. I love the Solidteknics brand for cooking over fire—they're made from 100 percent wrought iron and last a lifetime.*

Dutch Oven: *A bunch of these recipes call for a good Dutch oven. Look for a generously-sized cast-iron pot, ideal for slow-roasting and baking over fire.*

Grate: *A grate allows you to elevate your pots and pans above the coals and grill your bread.*

Portable Gas Stove: *The ultimate camping companion! This cooker combines a lightweight gas canister with the heat needed to cook a meal. You can find them at most good camping stores.*

Tripod: *A tripod helps suspend your pots and pans over a heat source. I prefer a metal camping tripod, but you can also make one out of driftwood (see page 112).*

S-Hook: *Small enough to keep in your back pocket, this handy hook helps rig up food over a fire. Most good butcher's shops will have them or scout your local cooking store.*

Cooking Stand: *This helpful tool provides the lift you need to cook over fire without smothering the flame and it lets you slowly cook food without the risk of burning.*

Jaffle (Pie) Iron: *These cast-iron toasted sandwich presses are so much fun to use. After all, you can't cook a bread and butter toastie without a jaffle iron! (See pages 67 and 69 for the recipes.)*

Make-Shift Spatula: *This one's a cooking hack. I use a metal paint scraper to flip, chop, and move things around in a frying pan. It offers great surface space and is super affordable. Use the sharp edge to chop your veg! (See pages 115 and 121)*

Enamelware: *Cups, plates, and cutlery that wash well and are virtually indestructible come in handy when cooking outdoors, especially if you've got kids running around!*

Shovel: *I find using a shovel while cooking and digging out my pit really handy. A medium-sized one should meet all your needs.*

PLAY-HOUSE

Let's be honest: None of us really want to grow up. Peter Pan got that much right. This chapter is inspired by Neverland and the world you can create in nature with a little imagination. I have the best memories of a weekend my family spent in New Zealand, where we kids made skirts out of reeds and spears out of sticks. We ran around as if we were hunting and created castles in trees and cubby houses in the forest. These recipes encourage kids (and adults!) to see the world with fresh eyes, as we forage for wildflowers to decorate toffee apples and bake self-saucing chocolate pudding in hollowed-out coconuts.

SNACK ATTACK

This is a great recipe to make with your kids in the morning, so it's ready for snack time. I also like to cook it at home, in the oven, and take it on hikes. If you want to do so, preheat the oven to 350°F (180°C), press the mixture into a parchment paper–lined 8-inch (20 cm) baking pan, and bake for about 30 minutes.

Makes 12

2 cups (200 g) rolled oats

1 cup plus 1 tablespoon (140 g) all-purpose flour

1 cup (200 g) granulated sugar

1 cup (85 g) dried shredded coconut

1 cup (130 g) dried apricots, chopped

1 cup (140 g) almonds, chopped

1 tablespoon ground cinnamon

1 cup plus 2 tablespoons (255 g) unsalted butter

½ cup (120 ml) honey

½ cup (120 ml) rice malt syrup

½ teaspoon baking soda

Light your fire and let it burn down for about 1 hour, or until you obtain a medium heat. Build a tripod over the top. Line the bottom and sides of a Dutch oven with parchment paper.

Combine the oats, flour, sugar, coconut, apricots, almonds, and cinnamon in a large bowl.

Melt the butter in a medium saucepan. Add the honey and rice malt syrup and cook over medium heat for about 2 minutes, or until bubbling. Add ½ cup (125 ml) of water and bring to a boil then remove from the heat and add the baking soda. Add to the oat mixture and mix well.

Press the mixture into the parchment-lined Dutch oven and put the lid on. Place on the tripod set over the fire, shovel some more coals on top, and bake for about 20 minutes, or until firm to the touch and golden brown around the edges. Carefully remove the Dutch oven from the fire and allow to cool completely. Cut into 12 pieces and serve.

HOT FRUIT

In the summer, fresh stone fruit is abundant and wonderfully juicy, but sometimes it's still nice to cook with it. When I'm not baking stone fruit into a cake, this simple recipe is my go-to. Don't be alarmed by the amaretto—the alcohol evaporates during cooking, leaving behind a delicious almond flavor. If you'd rather not use it, replace it with apple juice.

Serves 6

1 cup (200g) granulated sugar

6 figs (or other stone fruit, such as plums or peaches), halved and pits removed

1 cup (240 ml) amaretto

Cream Dream (page 53)

Light your fire and let it burn down for about 1 hour, or until you obtain a medium heat.

Heat a medium-sized cast-iron frying pan over a grill on the fire until smoking hot. Sprinkle the sugar into the pan, then immediately add the stone fruit, cut-side down, and cook for about 3 minutes, or until the sugar starts to bubble and caramelize. Add the amaretto and stand back a little. It will flame for a couple minutes until the alcohol cooks off. Flip the fruit over and cook for about 5 minutes, or until soft, juicy, and a little charred. Serve with Cream Dream (page 53).

FIRE SALAD

You can play around with the root vegetables and choose different varieties to hang over the fire. I love watching them swing over the flames, as their delicious cooking smells waft around the campsite.

Serves 4

4 medium red beets

4 medium carrots

4 spring onions

Salad leaves, for serving

Grated Parmesan or other sharp cheese, for serving

<u>Balsamic dressing</u>

2 cups (480 ml) balsamic vinegar

8 garlic cloves, crushed

1 bunch fresh thyme or rosemary

2 tablespoons extra-virgin olive oil

Salt and freshly ground black pepper

Butcher's string or garden wire

Light your fire and let it burn down for about 1 hour, or until you obtain a medium heat. Build a tripod over the top.

String the vegetables up using butcher's string or garden wire. Hang the beets over the fire, using the tripod, and cook for 1 hour, then hang the carrots and onions, and cook with the beets for another 2 to 3 hours, or until tender.

Meanwhile, make the dressing: Combine the balsamic vinegar, garlic, and thyme in a saucepan and bring to a boil over the fire on a grill. Continue boiling for about 15 minutes, or until the strong vinegar flavor mellows and the mixture is reduced by half. Let cool then strain into a bottle. Whisk in the olive oil and season with salt and pepper.

Peel the veggies and slice. Arrange on a plate with the salad leaves. Drizzle with some of the balsamic dressing, finish with a generous grating of cheese, and serve. Reserve remaining dressing for another meal.

S + P CHICKEN

For the spice mix

2 teaspoons ground white pepper

1 teaspoon brown sugar or granulated sugar

1 teaspoon salt

¼ teaspoon five-spice powder

For the marinade

1 tablespoon vegetable oil

3 garlic cloves, finely grated

2 teaspoons finely grated fresh ginger

2 teaspoons brown sugar or granulated sugar

½ teaspoon salt

For the chicken

1 pound (450 g) boneless, skinless chicken thighs or breasts, cut into 1-inch (2.5 cm) pieces

1 large egg, beaten

½ cup (60 g) cornstarch

⅓ cup (80 ml) vegetable oil

1 small bunch fresh basil, roughly chopped

It's fun to use nature as a cooking vessel rather than relying on a man-made frying pan. I thought it would be especially fun to share a simple recipe cooked on a rock! You'll love the chicken, sure, but it will make you look at rocks with a new appreciation.

Serves 4

Light your fire and let it burn down for about 1 hour, or until you obtain a medium heat.

Find your rock—it needs to be about 12 inches (30 cm) long and completely dry, so it doesn't explode in the fire!—and heat it in the coals of the fire for about 10 to 15 minutes.

Meanwhile, for the spice mix, combine the white pepper, brown sugar, salt, and five-spice powder in a small bowl and mix well.

For the marinade, combine the vegetable oil, garlic, ginger, brown sugar, and salt in a large bowl and mix well.

Add the chicken to the marinade and mix well to coat. Marinate for at least 30 minutes at room temperature, or overnight in a cooler.

When ready to cook, add the beaten egg to the marinated chicken and stir to mix well. Sprinkle with the cornstarch and press down so it forms an even coating on the chicken. The batter should be quite dry.

Once your rock is hot, add a splash of vegetable oil and allow to heat. Adding one piece at a time, fill the rock's surface with chicken, leaving an inch (2.5 cm) between each fillet. Cook for 2 to 3 minutes, or until golden brown on the bottom. Flip the chicken and cook for another 2 to 3 minutes, or until golden brown and cooked through on the other side. Repeat with remaining fillets until all are golden and cooked through. If you're using a large cast-iron frying pan instead of a rock, add just enough vegetable oil to coat the bottom and then place over the fire on a grate burning with medium–high heat.

Sprinkle about half the spice mix over the hot chicken and gently toss with a pair of tongs. Taste and add more spice mix as needed. Top with a generous handful of basil and serve.

SNITCHES!

This beautiful recipe works just as well with chicken if you can't find venison. If you're using chicken, make sure you choose boneless, skinless breasts that have been butterflied—ask your butcher for help or try it yourself!

Serves 4

4 medium-sized venison tenderloin steaks (1 ¾ pounds / 800 g) or boneless, skinless chicken breasts, butterflied

2 large eggs

1 cup (240 ml) whole milk

2 cups (180 g) panko breadcrumbs

1 cup (130 g) all-purpose flour

1 cup (120 ml) sunflower oil

Salt

Light your fire and let it burn down for about 1 hour, or until you obtain a medium heat.

Pound the venison steaks with a meat tenderizer to tenderize and flatten them out. (If using chicken, cut each breast in half then pound to tenderize and flatten.)

Whisk together the eggs and milk in a shallow bowl. Place the breadcrumbs and flour in 2 separate bowls. Dip each venison steak in the egg mixture, then dredge in the flour, patting to coat well. Dip each venison steak back in the egg wash, then dredge in the breadcrumbs, gently shaking off any excess.

Heat a large cast-iron frying pan in the coals of the fire, add all the sunflower oil, and heat until the venison sizzles when added to the pan. Cook the venison, flipping once, for 3 to 5 minutes, or until golden brown on both sides. If using chicken, cook the flattened chicken breast, flipping once, for 4 to 5 minutes, or until golden brown on both sides and cooked through. Season with salt and serve hot.

WHOLE ROASTED SQUASH

Whole squash and fire go hand in hand. An open fire has a higher heat than most electric ovens, which brings out the natural sugars in the butternut squash. If you don't finish this dish in one sitting (and that's a big if!), leftovers keep well for a cold salad the next day.

Serves 2

1 packet (7 ounces / 200 g) falafel mix

1 large (3 pounds) butternut squash

Fresh rosemary sprigs

Extra-virgin olive oil, for drizzling

Salt

Wavy Gravy (page 31)

Butcher's string or garden wire

Light your fire and let it burn down for about 1 hour, or until you obtain a medium heat.

Make your falafel mix according to the packet instructions.

Cut the squash lengthwise in half, scoop out the seeds, and stuff both halves with the falafel mix. Put the 2 halves back together and tie with string, then tuck the rosemary sprigs under the string or wire. Place the squash in a Dutch oven, drizzle generously with olive oil, and season with a good pinch of salt. Put the lid on the Dutch oven and arrange in the coals of the fire. Scoop some extra coals on top and cook for about 1 hour, or until the squash is soft.

Carefully remove the Dutch oven from the coals and let cool slightly then remove the squash, cut off the string, and serve with Wavy Gravy.

WAVY GRAVY

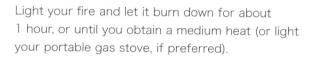

Gravy is a natural partner for many meat dishes, but I love to serve it alongside vegetables. This vegetarian gravy is a great addition to whole roasted squash, or any roast for that matter.

Makes about 1 cup (240 ml)

½ cup (30 g) nutritional yeast

2 tablespoons brown rice flour

1 ½ cups (360 ml) vegetable stock

⅓ cup (90 g) tahini

2 tablespoons soy sauce

Light your fire and let it burn down for about 1 hour, or until you obtain a medium heat (or light your portable gas stove, if preferred).

In a medium saucepan on a grate over the fire at medium heat, toast the nutritional yeast and brown rice flour over medium heat, stirring frequently, for 3 to 5 minutes, or until slightly browned and fragrant.

Add the vegetable stock, tahini, and soy sauce, whisking rapidly to combine and remove any lumps. Increase the heat to medium-high by moving the saucepan closer to the flames and cook until bubbling, then reduce the heat to low and simmer until thickened to your liking.

Serve immediately. Leftover gravy can be refrigerated in an airtight container for up to 7 days. This gravy thickens as it cools, so when you reheat it, add a little extra vegetable stock or water to loosen it.

SEA LETTUCE CUPS

I really think the kids will be into this recipe. Abalone is so unexpected, and it's good to mix it up and use ingredients that you wouldn't think of. It might also encourage your kids to broaden their culinary horizons and enjoy more variety in their diet. In Tasmania, we dive for abalone, but you can also find it at a good, sustainable fish shop. Of course, feel free to replace the abalone with prawns, more mushrooms, or some sweet potato if that's easier.

Serves 4

For the Sauce

1 ¼ teaspoons cornstarch

2 tablespoons soy sauce

2 tablespoons oyster sauce

2 tablespoons mirin

1 teaspoon sesame oil

For the Abalone

1 tablespoon sunflower oil

1 large garlic clove, minced

½ teaspoon minced fresh ginger

½ onion, finely chopped

1 small carrot, finely chopped

5 shiitake or other mushrooms, finely chopped

1 medium abalone (about 5 ounces / 150 g) or 8 king prawns

8 butter or iceberg lettuce leaves, washed and dried

Light your fire and let it burn down for about 1 hour, or until you obtain a medium heat.

To prepare the abalone, take it out of the shell and remove the guts and beak (I leave the frill on mine). Pound the abalone with a large rock to tenderize it, then slice as thinly as possible.

For the sauce, whisk the cornstarch with 1 tablespoon of water until smooth and lump free. Add the soy sauce, oyster sauce, mirin, sesame oil, and 2 tablespoons of water and whisk until well combined.

Increase the heat of the fire by adding more wood and letting it burn down slightly. For the abalone, heat the sunflower oil in a wok or large cast-iron frying pan on a grate, over high heat. Add the garlic and ginger and give it a quick stir, then add the onion and carrot and cook for 3 to 5 minutes, or until slightly softened. Add mushrooms and cook for about 2 minutes, or until the mushroom has softened.

Add the sauce and cook for 1 ½ minutes, or until it is thick and glossy. Add the abalone and cook for a further 2 minutes, then scoop into a serving bowl.

Lay out the lettuce leaves, then let everyone add their own filling and enjoy!

COOKED IN COCO

I really enjoy being creative with what nature gives us—and this recipe is a perfect example of using ingredients in a fun, resourceful way. Kids love the novelty of eating without a plate! You can also make it at home—just bake the coconuts in a 350°F (180°C) oven.

Serves 4

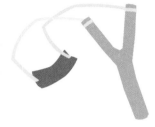

4 large green or young coconuts

2 cups (480 ml) coconut milk

1 cup (190 g) jasmine rice

1 pound (450 g) boneless venison or boneless, skinless chicken, cut into 1-inch (2.5 cm) pieces

1 small onion, finely diced

1 teaspoon curry powder

Salt and freshly ground black pepper

Sliced spring onion, chopped peanuts, and fresh cilantro leaves, for serving

Light your fire and let it burn down for about 1 hour, or until you obtain a medium heat.

Use a heavy butcher's knife to cut off the tops of the coconuts. Reserve the tops to use as lids. Pour the liquid from inside the coconuts as well as the additional coconut milk into a small saucepan and bring to a boil on a grill over the fire.

Place ¼ cup (48 g) of rice in each coconut, then divide the venison or chicken, onion, and curry powder evenly among the coconuts. Season with salt and pepper then evenly divide the boiling coconut milk into each coconut and stir to incorporate. Place the tops back on the coconuts and wrap each one in a double layer of aluminum foil. Place in the coals of the fire and bake for about 1 hour and 40 minutes, or until the venison or chicken is cooked through and the sauce is reduced. Carefully remove the foil and lids then top with sliced spring onion, chopped peanuts, and cilantro and enjoy!

CHOCONUT

I'm going through a real coconut phase at the moment, which is what led me to create this slightly tropical twist on good old-fashioned chocolate pudding. So good!

Serves 4

4 large green or young coconuts

1 cup (240 ml) coconut milk

1 cup (125 g) self-rising flour

1 cup (200 g) superfine (caster) sugar

½ cup (60 g) cocoa powder, plus more for dusting

¼ cup (60 g) unsalted butter, melted and cooled

2 large eggs

½ teaspoon pure vanilla extract

Light your fire and let it burn down for about 1 hour, or until you obtain a medium heat.

Use a heavy butcher's knife to cut off the tops of the coconuts. Reserve the tops to use as lids. Pour the liquid from inside the coconuts as well as the additional coconut milk into a small saucepan and bring to a boil over the fire. Set aside to cool slightly.

Sift the flour, half of the superfine sugar, and half of the cocoa powder into a bowl and stir to combine. Make a well in the center.

Add the melted butter, eggs, and vanilla to the cooled coconut milk and whisk until smooth. Gradually pour into the flour mixture and fold to combine.

Rinse out the saucepan and bring 1 cup (240 ml) of water to boil on a grate over the fire.

Divide the coconut and cocoa mixture evenly among the coconuts. Mix together the remaining superfine sugar and cocoa powder and sprinkle over the puddings. Carefully pour ¼ cup (60 ml) of the boiling water into each one.

Place the tops back on the coconuts and wrap each one in a double layer of aluminum foil. Place in the coals of the fire and bake for about 40 minutes, or until the tops of the puddings are firm. Carefully remove the foil and lids then sprinkle with cocoa powder and serve.

EGGCELLENT STEAKS

Eggplant has a reputation for being tricky to cook, so it may not be everyone's first choice. But, if you're after some inspiration, give this recipe a try for an exciting meat-free alternative on your family picnic table. I love to serve these "steaks" with Coolslaw and hot sauce.

Serves 4

4 large eggplants

2 large eggs

1 cup (240 ml) whole milk

2 cups (180 g) panko breadcrumbs

1 cup (130 g) all-purpose flour

½ cup (125 ml) ghee

Salt

Coolslaw (page 41) and hot sauce, to serve

Light your fire and let it burn down for about 1 hour, or until you obtain a medium heat.

Place the eggplants in the coals, near the outer edges of the fire, as you want to cook the flesh but not burn it. Cook for 3 to 5 minutes, or until softened, then remove and let cool completely. Carefully peel off the skin, removing as little flesh as possible, then place the eggplants on a cutting board.

Whisk together the eggs and milk in a shallow bowl. Place the breadcrumbs and flour in 2 separate bowls. Dredge the eggplants in the flour, patting to coat well, then dip in the egg mixture, followed by the breadcrumbs, gently shaking off any excess.

Heat a large frying pan in the coals of the fire and melt the ghee. Working in batches, fry the eggplant, flipping once, for 6 to 8 minutes, or until golden brown. Season with salt and serve with the Coolslaw and your favorite condiments, like hot sauce.

COOLSLAW

I often hang a whole cabbage over the fire, but this simpler method makes a delicious salad that kids love making and eating. Cooking the cabbage slowly over the fire brings out its natural sugars, making this mild vegetable a little sweeter.

Serves 6

1 green cabbage

1 cup (240 ml) plain yogurt

½ bunch fresh dill, chopped

Grated zest and juice of 1 lemon

Salt and freshly ground black pepper

1 cup (125 g) walnuts (or your favorite nut), toasted then lightly crushed

Light your fire and let it burn down for about 1 hour, or until you obtain a medium heat.

Cut the cabbage in half, lengthwise, and place, cut-side down, on a grate over the coals. Cook for about 30 minutes, or until well charred. Remove from the grate and thinly slice.

Combine the yogurt, dill, and the lemon zest and juice in a bowl and season with salt and pepper. Add the cabbage and toss to combine. Sprinkle with the walnuts and serve.

O-CAKE

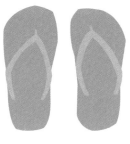

This is another handy recipe to have in your back pocket, as oranges are generally available all year round. The batter is super forgiving, and baking it over an open fire gives the cake a delicious smoky flavor I find perfect for afternoon tea. If you want to mix up the flavors, add a little chopped dark chocolate.

Serves 6

1 orange, unpeeled and roughly chopped

¾ cup (85 g) almond meal

½ cup (100 g) raw sugar, such as Demerara or Turbinado

1 teaspoon baking powder

3 large eggs

Light whipping (pouring) cream, for serving

For the syrup

Finely grated zest and juice of 2 oranges

½ cup (100 g) raw sugar, such as Demerara or Turbinado

Build a fire with lots of coals then light the fire and let it burn down for about 1 hour, or until you obtain a medium heat. Make sure there are still plenty of coals to cook over. Grease a Dutch oven and line the bottom and sides with parchment paper.

Place the roughly chopped orange in a medium saucepan and cover with water. Put the lid on the pan and cook over the fire on a grate for about 1 hour, or until the orange is tender. Drain off any excess water and mash the orange to a paste. Add the almond meal, raw sugar, baking powder, and eggs and stir until well combined. Pour the batter into the parchment-lined Dutch oven and spread it evenly to cover the bottom. Put the lid on the Dutch oven then place it in the coals of the fire and shovel some more coals on top. Bake for about 20 minutes, or until a skewer inserted in the center of the cake comes out clean. Carefully remove the Dutch oven from the fire, take off the lid, and let the cake cool in the Dutch oven.

Meanwhile, for the syrup, combine the orange zest and juice with the raw sugar and ½ cup (120 ml) of water in a small saucepan and bring to a boil over the fire. Continue boiling for 4 to 6 minutes, or until the sugar is dissolved and the syrup is slightly thick.

Once cool, remove the cake from the Dutch oven. Pour the hot syrup over the cake, slice and serve with a drizzle of cream.

APPLE-TOFFS

This is a fun recipe to make with kids around the campfire as a treat—toffee apples, my way! Decorating with wildflowers or herbs is a great way to teach them about edible flowers and lets them get creative as they personalize their own toffee apples. Briefly cooking the apples in water removes any wax on the skin, so the toffee sticks better. Make sure your sticks are sturdy enough and long enough to hold the apples over the fire.

Makes 6

6 apples

2 ½ cups (500 g) granulated sugar

2 cups (480 ml) cherry or apple cider

Fennel seeds and flaky salt

Dried marigold (calendula) flowers or fresh herbs, for decorating

6 long, sturdy sticks

Light your fire and let it burn down for about 1 hour, or until you obtain a medium heat.

Place a large pot of water on the grate over the fire and bring to a boil. Add the apples and cook for 2 to 3 minutes, or until slightly softened. Carefully remove the apples and dry them well.

In a medium saucepan, on the grate over the fire, combine the sugar and cider and gently bring to a simmer. Don't let the mixture boil—you want it to reach about 300°F (150°C). If it's too hot, add a splash of cold water to lower the temperature. Carefully remove from the heat and season with fennel seeds and salt. Don't be too heavy-handed with the fennel seeds—they have a strong flavor.

Insert a stick into each apple, making sure it has a firm fit. Swirl each apple through the toffee until well coated, letting any excess drip off. Decorate with flowers or herbs and leave to cool completely and set before serving.

LITTLE WOMEN

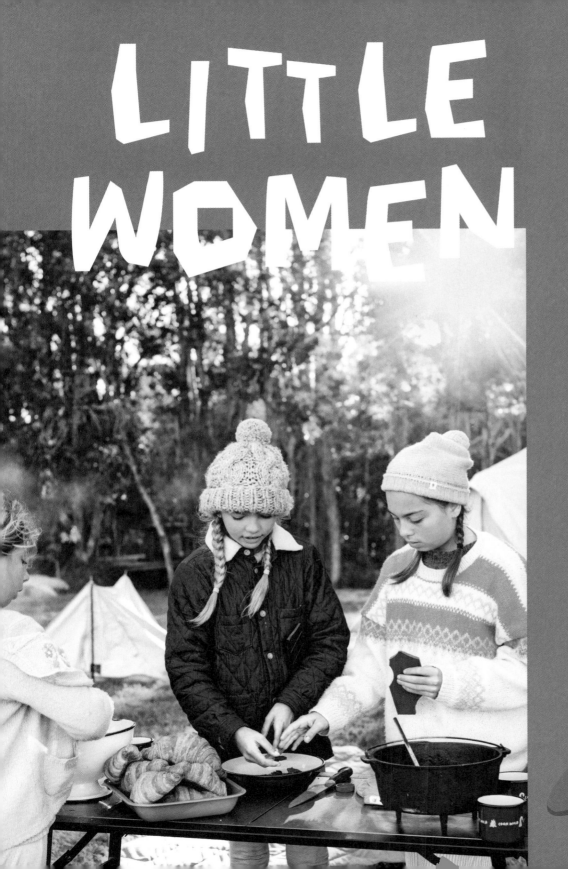

As a little girl, I was always trying to keep up with my brothers, taking every opportunity to join them on camping trips with Dad. I never understood why the great outdoors were only considered a man's domain. This chapter shows that camping isn't just hunting and roughing it. It can be a beautiful, feminine experience and a source of inspiration for mums and their daughters, too. I'm particularly fond of the sweet recipes in this chapter—we roast bananas over flames to make camp bananas, serve campfire crêpes with caramel sauce, and even bake an almond cake in the coals then top it with my favorite stone fruits and a little rosemary.

KID CRÊPES

When I was a kid, my brothers and I would compete with each other, trying to think of the most interesting flavors we could put on top of crêpes. This was not one of those ideas, but I bet I would have won, hands down, if I'd thought of this dulce de leche caramel filling when I was twelve!

Serves 4

1 (14-ounce / 395 g) can sweetened condensed milk, label removed

1 cup (130 g) all-purpose flour

2 cups (480 ml) whole milk

3 large eggs

Ghee or unsalted butter, for cooking

Heavy or thickened cream, for serving

Fill a large saucepan with enough water to completely cover the can of condensed milk (do not add the can yet) and bring to a rolling boil over the fire on a grate or on a portable gas stove. Carefully add the can and use tongs or a slotted spoon to submerge it in the boiling water, making sure to place the can on its side, so it can roll around. (If the can rests on its top or bottom, the boiling water can cause it to bounce up and down, which is really annoying.) Boil the can for 3 hours, without a lid on the saucepan, checking regularly to make sure the can is covered with water at all times and adding more boiling water as needed to ensure the can is covered.

Using tongs or a slotted spoon, carefully remove the can from the saucepan, place it on a heat-proof surface, and let cool to room temperature—dulce de leche firms up as it cools. Make sure it cools to room temperature before you open it, or the dulce de leche will squirt out like a fountain. Open the can and stir until smooth. Dulce de leche can be prepared ahead, cooled, and refrigerated in an airtight container for up to 3 weeks.

Now, let's get those crêpes happening.

Light your fire and let it burn down for about 1 hour, or until you obtain a medium heat.

Sift the flour in a bowl. Whisk together the milk and eggs in a jug, then add to the flour and whisk until well combined.

Heat a medium frying pan over medium heat on a grate over the coals or on a portable gas stove. Add 1 teaspoon of ghee and swirl it around until it melts. Add about 2 tablespoons of batter to the pan and swirl it around until it covers the base. Cook for 2 to 3 minutes, or until bubbles appear on the surface. Flip the crêpe then spoon some of the dulce de leche across the center and fold both sides over to cover it. Transfer to a plate and let rest to melt the caramel before serving. Repeat with the remaining batter and dulce de leche, then serve with a good drizzle of cream.

CAMP BANANAS

Quick and fun, this is probably one of the easiest campfire desserts you will ever make. Plus, kids love seeing the bananas cook and caramelize in front of their eyes. You're placing the bananas straight onto the fire, so make sure the adults help with cooking.

Serves 4

4 bananas

1 cup (150 g) large, flat chocolate discs or buttons

⅓ cup (75 g) superfine (caster) sugar

Cream Dream (page 53), for serving

Light your fire and let it burn down for about an hour, or until you obtain a hot heat—you need a hot fire to caramelize the sugar.

Grab a banana and tear off a strip of the skin, exposing some of the flesh. Repeat with the remaining bananas. Gently press the chocolate buttons around the side of each banana, so they stick inside the skin (this will allow the chocolate to melt without burning in the fire). Coat the exposed strip of banana flesh with superfine sugar; it will melt in the heat of the fire and turn to toffee, so you'll want to add a generous amount—more sugar means more delicious toffee.

Using a pair of long tongs, arrange the bananas under a burning log or really hot coals, which will act as a blowtorch on the sugar. Leave to cook in the fire for 2 to 5 minutes, or until the sugar has melted into toffee. Remove the caramelized bananas with the tongs, let cool briefly, and serve with Cream Dream.

CREAM DREAM

I'm not sure how I invented this recipe. I think I needed to make a sweet cream and didn't have enough regular cream, so I added mascarpone. Ever since, it has been one of my favorite additions to my desserts—it's creamy but not airy, sweet but not sugary, and it has a hint of vanilla that will have you licking the bowl.

Makes about 1 cup (240 ml)

½ cup (120 ml) heavy cream

½ cup (120 g) mascarpone

1 tablespoon raw sugar, such as Demerara or Turbinado

1 teaspoon vanilla bean paste

Combine the cream, mascarpone, raw sugar, and vanilla bean paste in a medium bowl and whisk just until starting to thicken ever so slightly. Cover and refrigerate for at least 30 minutes to allow the sugar to dissolve into the cream. Whisk again to incorporate all the melted sugar—it should be a very light brown color—before serving. Cream Dream can be refrigerated in an airtight container for up to 2 weeks.

PIGS + HONEY + ORANGES

The nice thing about this bacon is that you can enjoy it in savory or sweet dishes. The orange glaze offers a refreshing contrast to the richness of the salty bacon, which is great alongside breakfast, though I sometimes like to just eat it on its own.

Serves 4

Juice of 2 oranges

½ cup (120 ml) honey

Small handful fresh rosemary or thyme sprigs

8 slices bacon

Combine the orange juice, honey, and rosemary or thyme in a small saucepan and bring to a boil over the fire on a grate. Simmer for 5 minutes, or until some of the liquid evaporates and the glaze starts to thicken a little.

Place the bacon on a grate over the fire, brush with the orange glaze, and cook for 30 to 60 seconds. Flip the bacon over then brush with more orange glaze and cook for 30 to 60 seconds. Continue cooking and turning the bacon until cooked to your liking—I make mine crispy. Set aside to cool and harden slightly. Serve as is or with your favorite dish.

SWEET SMASH

You can eat these potatoes soft, right from the foil if you want, but I like to finish mine in a cast-iron frying pan to make them crispy. Serve this as a side with fish or chicken, or on its own as a sweet potato salad. You get the idea.

Serves 4

3 medium sweet potatoes

½ cup (120 ml) extra-virgin olive oil

Salt

1 tablespoon ghee or extra-virgin olive oil

Light your fire and let it burn down for about 1 hour, or until you obtain a medium heat.

Place the sweet potatoes in a bowl or on a cutting board, add the olive oil, and season with salt. Rub the oil all over the potatoes, then wrap them individually in aluminium foil, making sure the foil is well sealed, as you are going to put the potatoes in the coals of the fire and you want to protect them from dirt and so on. Place in the coals and cook, turning every 15 minutes with tongs or a tea towel, so you can feel the potatoes, for about 30 to 40 minutes total, or until soft and cooked through. Carefully remove the foil.

Heat a cast-iron frying pan in the coals and melt the ghee. Break up the sweet potatoes, add to the frying pan, and cook, flipping the potatoes gently so they don't break up too much and seasoning with salt as you go, for about 6 to 8 minutes, or until caramelized. Add a little more salt and enjoy.

TOMMY SAL

I love tomatoes cooked in fire—they become juicy and sweet, and their acidity pairs perfectly with any choice of protein, though I particularly like them with fish. Kids will have a lot of fun preparing this dish.

Serves 6

½ cup (95 g) long-grain jasmine or basmati rice

1 small shallot, chopped

½ cup (70 g) almonds, roughly chopped

2 tablespoons currants

Finely grated zest of 1 lemon

1 ½ tablespoons unsalted butter

1 teaspoon ground cumin

Salt and freshly ground black pepper

6 large tomatoes

Extra-virgin olive oil, for drizzling

½ cup (75 g) crumbled goat's milk feta

2 tablespoons roughly chopped fresh flat-leaf parsley

Light your fire and let it burn down for about 1 hour, or until you obtain a medium heat.

Boil the rice for 15 minutes, or until it is slightly underdone. Drain, then while the rice is still warm, add the shallot, almonds, currants, lemon zest, butter, and cumin. Season with salt and pepper and mix well.

Slice off and reserve the tops of the tomatoes, scoop out the flesh, and roughly chop it. Stir into the rice mixture then spoon the filling evenly into the scooped-out tomatoes.

Place the tomatoes in a single layer in a Dutch oven, drizzle with a little olive oil, and season with salt and pepper. Place the tomato tops back on top of the tomatoes then cover with the lid of the Dutch oven. Carefully place the Dutch oven in the coals of the fire, shovel some more coals on top, and cook for 20 to 30 minutes, or until the tomatoes are soft. Remove the lid of the Dutch oven and cook for another 10 minutes. Carefully remove the tomatoes and place on a platter. Sprinkle with the feta and parsley and serve.

FIRE CAKE

This cake has become an essential feature of most of my campfire dinner parties, but it's also perfect for afternoon tea or even breakfast. You can use almost any fruit on top, so it's great for any season.

Serves 6

¾ cup plus 1 tablespoon (190 g) unsalted butter, softened

1 cup (210 g) raw sugar, such as Demerara or Turbinado

2 large eggs

¾ cup (180 ml) buttermilk (or whole milk plus a squeeze of lemon juice)

1 cup plus 2 tablespoons (150 g) all-purpose flour

⅔ cup (75 g) almond meal

2 teaspoons baking powder

6 apricots, halved and pitted

1 to 2 fresh rosemary sprigs (optional)

Cream Dream (page 53) or light whipping (pouring) cream, for serving

Light your fire and let it burn down for about 1 hour, or until you obtain a medium heat. Build a tripod over the top. Line an 8-inch (20 cm) Dutch oven with parchment paper.

Beat the butter and raw sugar until soft and creamy (if it won't cream, don't stress—it will still turn out fine). Add the eggs, 1 at a time, and beat until incorporated. Add the buttermilk, followed by the flour, almond meal, and baking powder and mix with a wooden spoon until combined. Pour the batter into the parchment-lined Dutch oven and arrange the apricot halves on top any way you like. Finish with the rosemary, if using, and cover with the lid of the Dutch oven. Place on the tripod set over the fire, shovel some more coals on top, and bake for 15 to 30 minutes, or until the cake is firm to the touch and bounces back when lightly pressed. Carefully remove the Dutch oven from the fire and let cool for 10 minutes. Remove the cake from the Dutch oven and slice, serving the cake with Cream Dream or light whipping cream.

TONS OF SCONES

I like the idea of busting the myth that you can't make pastry over a campfire. Kids love to bake, and scones are fun, because you can really get in there with your hands. Don't worry about the beer—it just acts as a rising agent and adds a nice savory note, but you could use milk instead if preferred. All in all, this is a very satisfying way to spend an afternoon around the fire.

Makes 12 scones

⅓ cup plus 1 teaspoon (80 g) unsalted butter, chilled and cut into cubes, plus more for serving

3 cups (375 g) self-rising flour, plus more for dusting

1 cup (95 g) grated Parmesan or other sharp cheese

1 tablespoon chopped fresh chives

1 cup (240 ml) stout or other dark beer, plus more as needed

Light your fire and let it burn down for about 1 hour, or until you obtain a medium heat. Build a tripod over the top. Lightly dust a Dutch oven with flour.

In a large bowl, use your fingertips to rub the butter into the self-rising flour until the mixture resembles fine breadcrumbs. Make a well in the center. Add the Parmesan, chives, and stout and mix with a knife to form a soft dough, adding more stout as needed and being careful to not overmix the dough, so the scones stay light rather than tough and heavy.

Turn out the dough onto a lightly floured surface and gently bring it together. Pat the dough into a 1-inch (2.5 cm) thick round. Using a 2-inch (5-cm) round cutter or mug (whatever is on hand), cut the dough into scones. Gently press the dough scraps together and cut out the remaining scones.

Place the scones, in a single layer, side by side but not touching, in the prepared Dutch oven. Sprinkle the tops with a little flour, then put the lid on the Dutch oven. Place on the tripod set over the fire, shovel some more coals on top, and bake for 15 to 20 minutes, or until the scones are golden and well risen. Carefully remove the Dutch oven from the fire and serve the scones warm, spread generously with butter.

YUMMY GREENS!

This broccoli is super versatile and a camp favorite. It makes a perfect dinner for two, or a great side dish. You can also break the broccoli into florets and toss them with rice or pasta—anything you like!

Serves 2 (or more as a side dish)

½ cup (120 ml) lemon juice, plus more for serving

2 tablespoons tahini, well stirred

2 tablespoons almond or peanut butter

3 large garlic cloves, minced

1 teaspoon soy sauce

Freshly ground black pepper

1 head broccoli, cut into florets

Light your fire and let it burn down for about 1 hour, or until you obtain a medium heat. Build a tripod over the top. Line a Dutch oven with parchment paper.

In a small bowl, combine the lemon juice, tahini, almond or peanut butter, garlic, soy sauce, and a few good grinds of pepper and mix well. Pour over the broccoli and massage into the florets.

Place the broccoli in the parchment-lined Dutch oven and put the lid on. Place on the tripod set over the fire, shovel some more coals on top, and cook for 10 to 20 minutes, or until the stalks are tender and the florets are crispy. Carefully remove the Dutch oven from the fire and serve the broccoli as you like.

BREAD + BUTTER TOASTIES

I often head to a bakery before I go camping, and don't always know what to do with leftovers. Well, here you go: These toasties are the perfect solution. In fact, they are so good that you'll be tempted to buy a bunch of croissants and let them go stale on purpose.

Serves 4

3 large eggs

1 cup (240 ml) whole milk

½ cup (100 g) coconut sugar

1 teaspoon ground cinnamon

4 fresh or day-old croissants

1 tablespoon unsalted butter, melted

4 jaffle (pie) irons

Light your fire and let it burn down for about 1 hour, or until you obtain a medium heat.

Place the eggs, milk, coconut sugar, and cinnamon in a bowl and whisk until combined. Tear the croissants into bite-sized pieces and add to the mixture, gently pressing, so the croissants absorb the liquid.

Brush the jaffle irons with melted butter. Add a pile of the croissant mixture to each iron, then put the lids down and fold shut. Place the irons in the coals of the fire for about 5 minutes, or until the mix is crisp and golden. Take the irons out of the fire and let cool slightly before serving.

B'FAST TOASTIES

I like old-school white bread when making toasties—sandwiches pressed together with cheese and other fillings in the middle—but sourdough is also delicious and better for you. Then again, I'm not sure you can call a sandwich full of mayo and cheese healthy. Everything in moderation, I say!

Serves 6

1 (15-ounce / 425 g) can organic baked beans

½ cup (113 g) whole-egg mayonnaise

1 loaf white or other bread, thickly sliced

1 ⅓ cups (150 g) grated mozzarella

6 slices jamón or other ham

4 large eggs

4 jaffle (pie) irons

Light your fire and let it burn down for about 1 hour, or until you obtain a medium heat.

Heat the beans in a small saucepan on a grate over the fire and set aside.

Spread a layer of mayonnaise on both sides of the bread slices. Add a layer of mozzarella and jamón to half the bread slices, then place in the jaffle irons.

Crack the eggs into a bowl and beat until creamy. Cook the eggs over the fire, Spoon a little scrambled egg over the jamón and top with the warm beans. Top with the remaining bread slices, quickly put the lid down and fold shut. Place the irons in the coals of the fire for about 5 minutes, or until the cheese has melted and the egg is cooked.

Take the irons out of the fire, crack them open, and enjoy your breakfast!

SIBELLA + THE PIRATES

What do you get when you invite iconic Australian stylist, Sibella Court, and a buccaneering crew of kids to River Hawk for a weekend of fun? A whole load of Swiss Family Robinson–style adventure, that's what. I've known Sibella for years and have always admired her childlike curiosity and creative spirit. It was a dream to create this adventure—teaching kids how to cook and thrive in nature with a hand-built raft, just-caught mussels, and seriously good lobster sandwiches (don't knock 'em until you try 'em!).

LOBSTER ROLLOVERS

These lobster rolls are a treat to make and remind me of summer and diving for crayfish and lobster with my brothers. We'd light a fire to make rolls and fill them with delicate creamy meat from the sea.

Serves 4

2 (3-pound / 1.4 kg) medium lobsters or Moreton Bay bugs

½ cup (125 g) melted ghee

2 garlic cloves, finely chopped

⅓ cup (75 g) whole-egg mayonnaise, plus more for serving

2 sprigs (or stems) each of fresh flat-leaf parsley, mint, and chives, finely chopped

Finely grated zest and juice of 1 lemon and 1 lime

Salt and freshly ground black pepper

4 Salty Rolls (page 75) or top-split, flat-sided hotdog buns

4 leaves Boston or other lettuce

Your favorite pickles, for serving

Light your fire and let it burn down for about 1 hour, or until you obtain a medium heat.

Meanwhile, put your lobsters to sleep in a bucket of ice with a lid on it. This will take about 1 hour or so.

Slice each lobster in half from head to tail, brush with some ghee, and place, flesh-side down, on the grate over coals. Cook for 5 minutes, then flip the lobsters, brush with more ghee, sprinkle with the garlic, and cook for another 5 minutes, or until the flesh is cooked through. Remove from the heat and let rest for 5 minutes.

Pull the lobster meat out of the shells and place in a bowl. Add the mayonnaise, parsley, mint, chives, 1 tablespoon of lemon juice, lemon and lime zest, and gently toss to coat—the lobster should be lightly coated, but not weighed down by the mayo. Taste the lobster salad. Some brands of mayo have more tang than others; if the salad needs more brightness, add a squeeze each of lemon and lime juice. Season with salt and pepper.

Spread some mayo on the inside of each roll or bun and grill for 1 to 2 minutes per side, or until toasted to your liking. Place a lettuce leaf in each bun, then fill with a generous mound of lobster salad, top with pickles, and serve.

SALTY ROLLS

If you are on the beach, why not make these rolls with ocean water? Just be sure to bring the water to a rapid boil for five minutes first. If not, regular fresh water is fine—just add a teaspoon of salt to every cup (240 ml) of water to replicate salty seawater. These rolls are left to rise in a warm spot—try somewhere sunny and protected from wind.

Serves 4

3 cups (390 g) all-purpose flour

1 ½ cups (360 ml) boiled ocean water, plus more as needed, cooled to a warm temperature

1 (¼-ounce / 7 g) envelope active dry yeast

Extra-virgin olive oil, for drizzling

Thinly sliced garlic (optional)

Place the flour in a large bowl and make a well in the center. Add the warm ocean water and yeast to the well then use your fingers to bring the dough together. Turn out the dough onto a floured surface and knead for 10 to 15 minutes, or until smooth and slightly sticky. If the dough is too dry, gradually add more warm ocean water. Shape into 4 rolls, then place on a floured stone rock or piece of driftwood, cover with a clean tea towel, and let rest in a warm spot for 1 hour, or until doubled in size.

Meanwhile, light your fire and let it burn down for about 1 hour, or until you obtain a medium heat.

Grab the dough and flatten each roll until about 1-inch (2.5 cm) thick. Toss the rolls directly in the coals of the fire and cook for 5 minutes, then use tongs to flip them over and cook for another 5 to 10 minutes, or until the bread sounds hollow when you tap it. Don't worry if the crust gets a little burnt—it just adds to the flavor! Serve the rolls straight out of the coals—make sure you dust off any dirt—with a good drizzle of olive oil and some sliced garlic, if you have a hankering for garlic bread.

MUSSEL COALS

As a kid, I used to walk on the rock shelves around Tasmania, with a bucket in tow for collecting mussels. It's really important to teach kids where their food comes from and how it grows. Mussels are a great introduction, as they are relatively easy to find and it's fun to show kids how to clean them. This recipe demonstrates just how little you need to do to make fresh ingredients shine.

Serves 4

1 ¾ pounds (800 g) mussels, cleaned and debearded

Freshly ground black pepper and/or finely chopped fresh flat-leaf parsley, for serving

Crème Fraîche Tartar Sauce (page 123), for serving

Light your fire and let it burn down for about 1 hour, or until you obtain a medium heat. When ready to cook, place a grate over the fire to cook the mussels on directly.

Add the cleaned mussels to the grate and cook for 5 to 10 minutes, or at least until they open. Some people like their mussels barely cooked and still soft and tender; others prefer them grilled until they're almost smoked, with the flesh condensed and almost crispy on the edges. Taste different levels of doneness and decide what you like! Discard any mussels that don't open.

Use tongs to transfer the hot mussels to a serving platter. While grilled mussels are just dandy as is, a few grinds of black pepper or a scattering of fresh parsley as you take them off the grill doesn't hurt. Once you have the open mussels on a serving platter, toss one or both over them then serve straight away with Crème Fraiche Tartar Sauce. The hotter and fresher, the better!

SEA PEARS

This is a handy recipe to have in your repertoire. Poached pears add a major wow factor to simple salads, and I particularly like them with arugula (rocket) and cheese, finished with a little balsamic dressing. Or, as we do here, you can enjoy them for dessert. Your choice!

Serves 4

4 cups (960 ml) ocean water (or 4 cups / 960 ml fresh water plus 2 teaspoons salt)

2 cups (400 g) superfine (caster) sugar

5 star anise

5 cinnamon sticks

4 pears

Cream Dream (page 53), for serving

Light your fire and let it burn down for about 1 hour, or until you obtain a medium heat. Build a tripod over the top.

Combine the ocean water, superfine sugar, star anise, and cinnamon in a large pot. Add the pears then place the pot on the tripod and bring to a boil. Reduce to a simmer and continue cooking for 15 minutes, or until the pears are tender. Carefully remove the pot from the tripod and let the pears cool in the poaching liquid. Remove the pears from the poaching liquid and slice in half. Serve the poached pears with Cream Dream.

Note: If you want to serve these poached pears on a cheese plate with some fresh bread, cut them in half and sear them, cut-side down, in a hot cast-iron frying pan until well browned and caramelized.

STICKY BUNS

2 teaspoons active dry yeast

¼ cup (50 g) superfine (caster) sugar

½ cup (120 ml) lukewarm whole milk

1 cup (240 ml) lukewarm water

4 cups (520 g) all-purpose flour

¼ cup (60 g) unsalted butter, cut into cubes

1 large egg yolk

Billy Jam (page 83) and heavy or thickened cream, for serving

Confectioners' (icing) sugar, sifted, for dusting

Build a fire with lots of coals then light the fire and let it burn down for about 1 hour, or until you obtain a medium heat. Make sure there are still plenty of coals to cook over. Build a tripod over the top.

Meanwhile, combine the yeast and 1 teaspoon of the superfine sugar in a small bowl. Add the lukewarm milk and lukewarm water and stir together. Set aside for 10 to 15 minutes, or until frothy.

Sift the flour and the remaining superfine sugar into a large bowl. Add the butter and use your fingertips to rub it into the flour and sugar until the mixture resembles fine breadcrumbs. Make a well in the middle, add the yeast mixture and mix until a soft dough forms.

Turn out the dough onto a floured surface and knead for about 5 minutes, or until it takes shape. Place the dough in a lightly oiled bowl, cover with a clean tea towel, and let rest in a warm place for about 1 hour, or until doubled in size.

Dust a Dutch oven with flour.

Punch down the dough in the bowl, then knead on a floured surface for about 5 minutes, or until it bounces back when poked. Divide the dough into 12 equal portions, then knead each portion into a smooth round, about the size of a golf ball. Arrange in a single layer in the prepared Dutch oven, allowing a little room for spreading if possible, and let rest in a warm place for about 10 minutes, or until it has doubled in size.

Whisk together the egg yolk and 1 teaspoon of water and brush over the buns. Put the lid on the Dutch oven and place on the tripod set over the fire then shovel some more coals on top and bake for about 20 minutes, or until the buns are golden brown. Carefully remove the Dutch oven from the tripod then transfer the buns to a wire rack and let cool.

Slit open each bun and fill with about a tablespoon of jam and a good drizzle of cream. Dust with a little sifted confectioners' sugar and dive in.

BILLY JAM

The best thing about campfire jam made in a billyboil is that you eat it all at once, so you don't need to stress about making it set like normal jam. This means it's a lot more forgiving and it tastes delicious spooned straight from the pan onto your food.

Makes about 2 cups (480 ml)

10 ½ ounces (300 g) fresh strawberries (hulled) or raspberries

1 ½ cups (300 g) granulated sugar

Light your fire and let it burn down for about 1 hour, or until you obtain a medium heat.

Place the berries and sugar in a heavy-bottomed saucepan set on a grill over the campfire and stir to coat the fruit in the sugar. Continue cooking until the sugar is dissolved, then move the pan to a hotter part of the fire and bring to a boil. Continue boiling, stirring only occasionally, for about 10 minutes, or until the jam turns a rich red color.

Take the pan off the fire and set aside until ready to serve—the jam will thicken slightly on standing.

KIDS' CAMP

There's no such thing as the kids' table when you're out camping. We're all equals in the wild, especially after a big day of exploring, playing, and maybe a little napping. Kids love getting involved with cooking, always flocking to the campfire to see what's roasting in the coals. This chapter is full of fun ideas and activities—think necklaces made of dried pasta and cheesy "popcorn" packed with zucchini. It's like an arts and crafts class meets the great outdoors. Don't miss my blueberry birthday cake (see page 93)—a special creation for my mate Jax's second birthday. Consider this your excuse to get your friends and their families together for an epic camping trip.

SNAG IN A BAG

Kids like to eat with their hands, and we can all agree that doing the dishes when you're camping stinks. So here is a simple recipe for sausages (or snags, as we call them Down Under) that will keep everyone happy. No plates required.

Serves 2

1 medium sweet potato, unpeeled and cut into bite-size pieces

2 pork or vegetarian sausages

2 large zucchini

1 garlic clove, finely chopped

Extra-virgin olive oil, for drizzling

Salt

Light a portable gas stove.

In a small saucepan, cover the sweet potatoes with water and bring to a boil. Lower the heat and cook for about 30 minutes, or until tender. Drain the sweet potatoes.

Using a mandoline or julienne peeler, peel the zucchini into noodles. Set aside.

Heat a Dutch oven over medium heat. Add the sausages and cook, turning regularly, for about 10 to 12 minutes, or until caramelized and almost cooked through. Cut into bite-size pieces.

Tear off 2 (12-inch / 30 cm) lengths of parchment paper. Place half the sausage, sweet potato, zucchini, and garlic in the middle of each piece of parchment, drizzle with olive oil, and season with salt. Fold up the parchment to form 2 sealed parcels—the steam trapped inside will cook the ingredients.

Heat the Dutch oven over high heat until smoking hot. Add the parchment parcels, then turn off the heat and put the lid on the Dutch oven. Let cook in the residual heat for 10 minutes. Carefully remove the parcels from the Dutch oven and serve.

Z POP

This addictive snack fits perfectly in kids' backpacks, ready for a hike, or in the baskets on their bikes, as they zoom around the campground with friends. Once cooked, simply wrap in foil, pack and go!

Serves 4

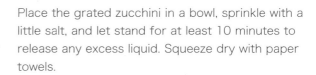

1 medium zucchini, grated

Salt

Extra-virgin olive oil, for frying

½ onion, finely chopped

1 garlic clove, finely chopped

2 tablespoons all-purpose flour

2 tablespoons grated cheddar cheese

1 large egg

Place the grated zucchini in a bowl, sprinkle with a little salt, and let stand for at least 10 minutes to release any excess liquid. Squeeze dry with paper towels.

Light a portable gas stove.

Heat a medium cast-iron frying pan over medium heat. Add a splash of olive oil, then sauté the onion and garlic for about 4 to 5 minutes, or until soft. Add the zucchini, then stir in the flour and cook for about 2 minutes, or until zucchini is cooked. Mix in the cheese and egg. Remove from the heat and let cool slightly, then shape the zucchini mixture into popcorn-sized pieces.

Wipe out the pan and pour in enough olive oil to coat the bottom. Add the zucchini "popcorn" and cook on medium heat for 2 to 3 minutes per side, or until golden brown all over. Remove with tongs or a slotted spoon and drain on paper towels. Transfer to a plate and let the kids dig in, or let cool and then wrap in foil to take on your next adventure.

POP TINS

Try to use self-opening cans for this, as they aren't sharp around the edges. If using regular cans, spoon the popcorn into a bowl so the kids don't hurt their little hands as they dig in.

Serves 6

⅓ cup plus 1 tablespoon (90 ml) olive oil

6 tablespoons popcorn kernels

Salt

6 empty food cans, well washed

Hammer

Nail

Rope

Aluminium foil

Use a hammer and a nail to punch 2 holes on opposite sides of each can, near the top. Carefully thread the rope through the holes to create a little handle. This one's a job for the adults!

Add 1 tablespoon of olive oil to each can, then add 1 tablespoon of popcorn kernels. Wrap the tops of the cans with aluminium foil to seal them shut.

Light a portable gas stove.

Place the cans over medium heat on the stove. As the oil heats up, the corn will start to pop. When the popping stops, carefully remove the foil and season with salt. Let the popcorn cool a bit before giving it to the kids.

BLUE BIRTHDAY CAKE

On this adventure, my gorgeous friend's baby, Jax, turned two and obviously we needed a cake! This may be news to you, but yes, you can make a cake on a camp stove—you are really steaming the cake rather than baking it. It's super delicious with blueberries, but you can use any ripe seasonal fruit here.

Serves 6

¾ cup (180 g) unsalted butter, softened

¾ cup (150 g) superfine (caster) sugar

1 teaspoon pure vanilla extract

2 large eggs

1 ½ cups (195 g) all-purpose flour

2 teaspoons baking powder

2 teaspoons ground cinnamon

½ cup (120 ml) whole milk

1 cup (145 g) blueberries

For the topping

1 tablespoon superfine (caster) sugar

1 teaspoon ground cinnamon

1 tablespoon unsalted butter, melted

In a large bowl, beat together the butter, superfine sugar, and vanilla until pale and creamy. Add the eggs, 1 at a time, beating well after each addition. Sift together the flour, baking powder, and cinnamon, then fold into the batter in 2 batches, alternating with the milk.

Light a portable gas stove. Line your Dutch oven with parchment paper. Place your Dutch oven on the stove and heat over medium heat until it is smoking hot. Remove the Dutch oven from the heat.

Spoon the batter into the parchment-lined Dutch oven, spreading evenly and smoothing the top, then dot with the blueberries. Put the lid on the Dutch oven and bake for 30 minutes—you can leave the Dutch oven off the heat for the first 10 minutes or so, but it will need to go back over low heat to finish baking the cake.

Meanwhile, for the topping, mix together the superfine sugar, cinnamon, and melted butter. Drizzle the topping over the cake while it's still warm and serve.

MUD CAKES

Mud isn't a dirty word. It's sweet and delicious and a little messy, but if you're on the beach or near a natural water source, the cleanup will be quick and easy.

Makes 12 cakes

1 cup (240 g) black beans, drained

½ cup (65 g) all-purpose flour

½ cup (100 g) coconut sugar

½ cup (70 g) Medjool dates, pitted and chopped

2 large eggs

1 tablespoon coconut oil

1 tablespoon cocoa powder

14 ounces (400 g) dark chocolate (at least 70%), broken into pieces

Unsweetened shredded coconut, for decorating

Light a portable gas stove. Heat a large Dutch oven over high heat. Once the Dutch oven is hot, reduce the heat to very low or turn it off—you need a low heat to cook these cakes without burning them.

Place the beans on a plate and let the kids mash them with their hands or a potato masher. Scoop the mashed beans into a large bowl then add the flour, coconut sugar, dates, eggs, coconut oil, and cocoa powder and mix well. The dough should look like mud.

Tear off a piece of parchment paper that is larger than the Dutch oven. Working in 2 batches of 6 cakes, dollop the mud cake batter onto the parchment like cookies, keeping them close to the center in a space no larger than the Dutch oven. Carefully transfer the parchment to the Dutch oven, so the cakes lie flat on the bottom. Put the lid on and bake for 5 minutes, then flip the cakes over and put the lid back on. If the gas stove is off, you may need to return it to low heat to finish cooking the cakes. Continue cooking for another 5 minutes, or until the cakes are cooked through. Carefully remove the cakes from the Dutch oven with the parchment paper, cool slightly then transfer the cakes to a plate. Reuse the paper and repeat the process with the remaining batch of cakes—you may need to reheat the Dutch oven.

Bring a saucepan of water to boil on a grate over the fire. Set a metal bowl over the simmering water and add the chocolate, stirring until melted. Take the melted chocolate and shredded coconut to the table and let the kids decorate their mud cakes. Enjoy immediately!

LAUGHING PIKELETS

I have such sweet memories of cooking in my childhood! I loved being playful in the kitchen and laughing at the sometimes unexpected results. This recipe for mini pancakes, which we call "pikelets" in Australia, encourages kids to experiment with food and lets them personalize their creations.

Serves 3

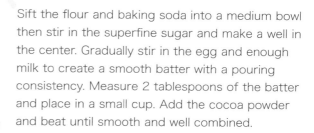

1 cup (125 g) self-rising flour

¼ teaspoon baking soda

¼ cup (50 g) superfine (caster) sugar

1 large egg, lightly beaten

1 cup (240 ml) whole milk

2 teaspoons cocoa powder

Unsalted butter, for cooking

½ cup (72 g) blueberries

Sift the flour and baking soda into a medium bowl then stir in the superfine sugar and make a well in the center. Gradually stir in the egg and enough milk to create a smooth batter with a pouring consistency. Measure 2 tablespoons of the batter and place in a small cup. Add the cocoa powder and beat until smooth and well combined.

Light a portable stove.

Place a large non-stick frying pan over medium heat. Add a little butter and when it melts, swirl the pan to coat the base. Pour a dollop of the plain batter into the pan to make a roughly 4-inch (10 cm) round pikelet, then use the cocoa batter to add a smile and 2 blueberries to add eyes. Cook for 1 to 2 minutes, or until bubbles appear on the surface, then flip the pikelet over and cook for another minute, or until golden. Use the rest of the batters and blueberries to make more pikelets, adding a little more butter between batches. Eat 'em while they're hot!

VEGGIE ROLLOVER

Easy and fun, these rollovers are a hands-on way for kids to help prep family meals. Serve them with dinner, or as a snack after they've run, hiked, or swam off their breakfast.

Serves 5

1 medium sweet potato, unpeeled and cut into bite-size pieces

5 large spinach leaves (not baby spinach)

Salt

Cheddar cheese, for grating

Light a portable gas stove.

In a small saucepan, cover the sweet potato with water and bring to a boil. Lower the heat and cook for about 30 minutes, or until tender. Let cool slightly then drain the sweet potatoes.

Lay the spinach leaves flat on a table then add the cooked sweet potato pieces and smash with your hands or a potato masher. Season with salt and grate over as much cheese as you want, then fold in the sides and roll up into parcels.

Place a large cast-iron frying pan over medium heat. Add the rollovers, seam-side down, and cook for 2 to 3 minutes then flip them over and cook for about 1 minute more, or until the sweet potato is hot and the cheese is melted.

Cut the rollovers into bite-size pieces or let the kids eat them whole or pull them apart with their hands.

PASTA NECKLACES

Think of this as a craft activity that turns into dinner. You could even give the kids little bowls of sauce for dipping their pasta necklaces into—maybe just take their shirts off first! Camping is all about getting grubby, right?

Makes 6

14 ounces (400 g) dried rigatoni or penne pasta

6 (20-inch / 50 cm) lengths of string

Place the pasta on a table or picnic blanket and let the kids thread it onto the string. Tie the ends to create a necklace, cutting off any excess string.

Light a portable gas stove.

Bring a large pot of salted water to boil over medium heat. Add the pasta necklaces and cook according to the package instructions until al dente. Transfer to a bowl of cold water, then drain on a piece of paper towel. Let the kids wear the necklaces and eat the penne as they play.

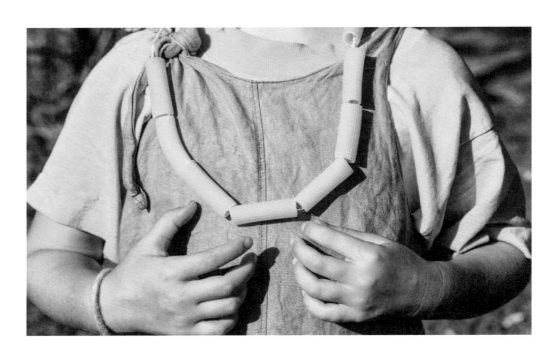

DOWN TO THE SEA

You've never met a more seaworthy crew than my thirteen-year-old mate, Arlo, and his inquisitive friends. Over the years, I've spent hours by the river, fishing with these boys and setting up campfires to cook what they catch. This chapter is as simple as it gets: showing kids how easy it is to cook fresh food without fancy equipment or even a frying pan. Instead, we rely on nature and a couple of basic tools. Using bamboo and string to suspend our catch over the coals creates a meal we can be really proud of making. Fish and chips cooked by the campfire? It's all in a day's work when you're out with Arlo.

FIRE FISH

Fish scales provide natural protection, so you don't need anything but a bed of coals to cook dinner. The smaller the fish, the better this method works—it's quick and simple.

Serves 4

1 line-caught whole white fish (4 pounds / 2 kg), such as sea bass

Turmeric Dressing (page 117) or ½ cup (120 ml) of your favorite dressing, for serving

Light your fire and let it burn down for about 1 hour, or until you obtain a medium heat.

Place the fish directly in the coals of the fire and cook for about 10 minutes, or until the skin is crispy. Carefully flip the fish over and cook for another 10 minutes, or until the flesh is cooked and the eyes are white.

Cut the top fillet from the fish then remove it with a spatula and cut it in half. Lift out the bones then remove the bottom fillet and cut it in half. Serve, drizzled with dressing.

PRAWNS ON STICKS

This is a really fun way to teach kids about preparing their own food. Send them off to find six sticks that are long enough to go over the fire—like you'd use for marshmallows—and use them as skewers for the prawns. This method also works well with other types of crustaceans, as well as other proteins or even vegetables.

Serves 6

1 cup (240 ml) Turmeric Dressing (page 117)

2 ½ tablespoons extra-virgin olive oil

Chile flakes, to taste

Salt, to taste

12 prawns, peeled and deveined

6 long, sturdy sticks

Combine the Turmeric Dressing, olive oil, chile flakes, and salt in a bowl, then add the prawns and massage to coat them in the mixture. Marinate for at least 1 hour.

Meanwhile, light your fire and let it burn down for about 1 hour, or until you obtain a medium heat.

Thread 2 prawns onto each stick and cook over the fire, turning regularly, for about 5 minutes, or until pink and cooked through. Cool slightly then eat!

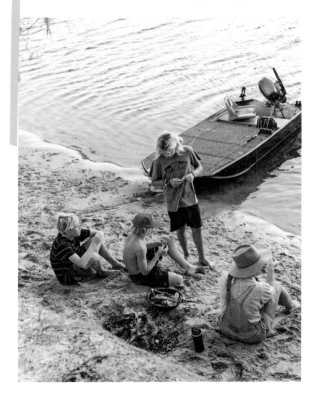

FISH ON
A STRING

Learning to identify ingredients growing naturally by the side of the road is a great way to show your kids that you don't have to go to the shops to buy everything. Pink peppercorn trees are abundant in Australia—they're also found in California, Hawaii, Florida, and South Africa—and their leaves have great flavor. Other edible plants to seek out include wild fennel and rosemary. Make a game of it and the kids can find dinner ingredients on the drive to your campsite.

Serves 4

4 to 6 small fish, such as small trout, sea bass, or snapper, cleaned and gutted

1 large handful fresh pink peppercorn leaves or wild fennel

Extra-virgin olive oil

Salt

Salty Smashed Spuds (page 111)

Butcher's string

Light your fire and let it burn down for about 1 hour, or until you obtain a medium heat. Set up a tripod over the top.

Stuff each fish with the peppercorn leaves or wild fennel. Tie some string around the fish to hold them together, then tie more string around the tails to create loops for hanging them.

Hang the fish from the tripod about 12 inches (30 cm) over the coals of the fire and cook for about 45 minutes, or until the flesh is cooked and the eyes are white.

Drizzle with olive oil, season with salt, and serve with Salty Smashed Spuds.

SALTY SMASHED SPUDS

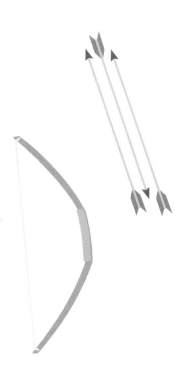

I love cooking food in ocean water when it's clean and safe to do so, because it adds an extra layer of flavor. It's also a fun way to show kids what it means to go straight to the source. And, by cooking this way, you don't need to season at the end! Lesson learned: Salt comes from the sea.

Serves 4

6 potatoes (about 2 pounds / 1 kg) good for making fries (chips), such as russet

Ghee, for frying

Boiled ocean water, or fresh water with one teaspoon of salt added to every 1 cup (240 ml) of water

Light your fire and let it burn down for about 1 hour, or until you obtain a medium heat. Build a tripod over the top.

In a medium saucepan, cover the potatoes with ocean water (or fresh water) and bring to a boil on a grate over the fire. Move the saucepan further from the heat to lower it and cook for 20 minutes, or until tender. Drain the potatoes then set on a tea towel and smash with your hands or a potato masher to flatten slightly.

Heat a frying pan on a grate over the fire, add 1 tablespoon of ghee, and let it melt. Add the smashed potatoes and cook, adding more ghee as needed, for 6 to 8 minutes, or until golden on the bottom. Turn the potatoes over and cook for another 5 minutes, or until golden on the other side. Serve with your favorite protein.

CORN ON A STRING

I'm not sure why I get such a kick out of hanging things in the air over a fire. You could cook the corn on a wire rack set over a fire, but where's the fun in that?

Serves 4

4 ears corn, husks on

½ cup (113 g) whole-egg mayonnaise

Unsalted butter, for serving

Salt

Butcher's string

Light your fire and let it burn down for about 1 hour, or until you obtain a medium heat. Build a tripod over the top.

Pull the husks most of the way off the corn, so they sit at the bottoms of the cobs. Braid the husks, then tie a loop of string to the ends. Coat the corn kernels in the mayonnaise.

Hang the corn about 8 inches (20 cm) over the flames and cook for about 30 minutes, or until the corn is tender and lightly charred. Enjoy with butter and salt.

NEWSPAPER FISH

I really want children to learn how to cook using their hands and only minimal equipment. We all know that newspaper can be used to light a fire, but sometimes it also makes a perfect cooking tool. You can use this method to cook any size fish.

Serves 4

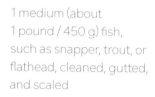

1 medium (about 1 pound / 450 g) fish, such as snapper, trout, or flathead, cleaned, gutted, and scaled

2 lemons, sliced

½ cup Turmeric Dressing (page 117) or your favorite dressing, for serving

20 sheets of newspaper

Light your fire and let it burn down for about 1 hour, or until you obtain a medium heat.

Wet the newspaper with water from the river or ocean (or tap water) then place it flat on a work surface, stacked, and put the fish in the middle. Stuff the fish with the lemon slices, then fold in the sides of the newspaper and roll up into a parcel.

Place the parcel in the coals of the fire and cook for 15 minutes then flip the parcel over and cook for another 15 minutes, or until the flesh is cooked and the eyes are white.

Let the fish rest in the newspaper for 5 minutes, then serve with Turmeric Dressing or your favorite dressing.

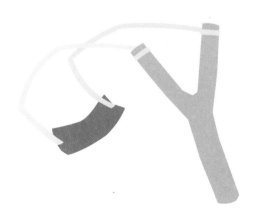

BAMBOO FISH

The idea here is that the radiant heat of the fire slowly cooks the fish, which is such a fun way to prepare your dinner, especially if you don't have a frying pan. Cooking in this primal, minimal way will give you a real sense of achievement and you can obviously add more fish if you are feeding a larger crowd. The dressing has a vibrant yellow color that looks great against the white flesh of the fish.

Serves 4

For the Turmeric Dressing

½-inch (1.25 cm) piece fresh turmeric, unpeeled

3 garlic cloves, peeled

½ cup (120 ml) Champagne vinegar

1 cup (240 ml) grapeseed or extra-virgin olive oil

4 bamboo shoots

4 small fish, such as snapper or flathead, cleaned and gutted but not scaled

1 large handful fresh lemon leaves or fresh herbs

Butcher's string or garden wire

For the turmeric dressing, finely grate the turmeric and garlic (use a Microplane, if you have one) into a small bowl. Add the vinegar and whisk until combined. Stir in the oil and let stand at room temperature for a few hours before serving.

Light your fire and let it burn down for about 1 hour, or until you obtain a medium heat.

Using a piece of wood or a knife, carefully whittle the tip of each bamboo shoot, so it's like a spear, then spear each fish with a bamboo shoot through the mouth and then up through the tail—you want the mouth to be about 12 inches (30 cm) from the base of the bamboo. Stuff each fish with lemon leaves or herbs, then tie each fish with butcher's string or garden wire, so it doesn't slide down the bamboo shoot.

Stick the bamboo spears into the ground about 8 inches (20 cm) away from the fire and in the direction of the wind. Push them about 4 inches (10 cm) into the ground to make sure they don't bend over into the fire or kiss the ground (see the photo for guidance). Cook for about 20 minutes, or until the skin starts to tighten and crisp up. Rotate the fish and cook for another 20 minutes, or until the flesh is cooked, skin is crisp, and the eyes are white.

Carefully remove the fish from the bamboo shoots and peel back the skin. Serve with the Turmeric Dressing.

FIRE FRUIT

When you heat up fruit, it takes on a different flavor, and when you heat it over a fire, it's infused with a subtle smokiness that's extremely appealing. This dish is great any time of day—all you need is a spoon. If you don't like or don't have access to pawpaw, try using pineapple and cook for a couple of minutes longer.

Serves 4

4 pawpaws or 4 small pineapples

½ cup (120 ml) maple syrup, plus more for drizzling

2 cups (480 g) coconut yogurt

4 limes

Light your fire and let it burn down for about 1 hour, or until you obtain a medium heat.

Slice the pawpaws in half and scoop out the bitter seeds. Place the pawpaws, cut-side up, in the coals of the fire, and drizzle the maple syrup in the center. Cook for 10 to 15 minutes, or until the flesh is soft and the maple syrup is bubbling. Carefully remove the pawpaws from the coals and top with the coconut yogurt. Squeeze some lime juice on top, drizzle with a little extra maple syrup, and serve.

SPUD
RÖSTI

Once you know how to cook rösti, it will quickly become a campfire favorite. It's perfect with eggs for breakfast, with freshly caught fish for dinner, or just as an afternoon snack.

Serves 4

6 unpeeled potatoes, such as russet

About ½ cup (100 ml) ghee

Salt

Light your fire and let it burn down for about 1 hour, or until you obtain a medium heat.

Place a heavy-bottomed frying pan in the coals to heat up.

Meanwhile, grate the potatoes onto a cutting board or plate. Melt 1 tablespoon of ghee in the pan, add all the potatoes, and use a spatula to gently flatten them into an even round, the size of the pan. Add a spoonful or so of ghee on top and cook for about 5 minutes, or until the bottom is golden brown. (You want a medium heat here—if the heat is too high, the potatoes will burn and if the heat is too low, they'll stew.) Flip the rösti, add more ghee if needed, and cook for another 5 minutes, or until crisp, golden, and cooked through. Season with salt and eat right away. YUM!

CRÈME FRAÎCHE TARTAR SAUCE

This quick and easy tartar sauce delivers the creaminess and acidity you need when eating fire-cooked fish or chicken. It's so good you'll want to add it to all your outdoor feasts.

Serves 4

1 cup (240 ml) crème fraîche

½ cup (100 g) chopped gherkins

1 tablespoon chopped capers

1 tablespoon chopped fresh flat-leaf parsley

Grated zest and juice of 1 lemon

Salt

Combine the crème fraiche, gherkins, capers, parsley, and the lemon zest and juice in a bowl and mix well. Season with salt. Let sit for 30 minutes, so the flavors can mingle.

INDEX

INDEX

INDEX

THANK YOU

A BIG thank you to everyone who made this book possible. What an effort to get it across the finish line. But we got there and what a book it is.

The motivation for this book came from a yearning to pay tribute to my childhood. Growing up, I would rush through my schoolwork (I was homeschooled) just so I could jump outside to join my brothers and the neighborhood kids on an adventure. These adventures were a highlight of my youth and formed much of my education and knowledge of the world.

Things have shifted in recent years and it's all too common to see kids spending time inside and not living in the outdoors as kids of my generation did. This book is a tribute to the imaginations of kids born in the 1980s, a time when we relied more on our imaginations, and were given the space and room to learn, create, and build without distraction. My aim for this book is to spark that imagination in a child's mind and encourage them outdoors.

I dedicate this book to my future children and to every child. The child that uses their imagination, that ventures out into nature, that creates memories with themselves and with others that will last a lifetime. It is my hope this book will contribute to creating lifelong memories between children, parents, families and friends that will last a lifetime and beyond.

Team Wild Child:

Kat Parker — Photographer. YOU MY DEAR, what a woman, what a talent. I'll forever be grateful to you for stopping by my cookie shop all those years ago. I have loved watching your career as a photographer blossom and this, well, it's really as much your book as mine. I love you.

Holly McCauley — Designer. For all your hard work designing this book and keeping it true to my heart. You're a joy to work with and your talent is eloquent.

Noa Amos — Artist. Your talent goes beyond your years, and your style is unique. Your future is so bright and this book "pops" and tells a story that could not be told without your artwork.

Steve, Kim, Noa, Hunter and Arlo Amos. Perhaps this book really should be "wild child RHR"? Really, who even are you? Angels from heaven? Thank you for always giving back to the arts and believing in me. I'm so thankful for our lifelong family friendship. I appreciate you both and I pray that every blessing you have bestowed upon me comes back 1,000 x 1,000-fold. I love you both.

Maddy Hadley. We have been friends for too long to admit for fear of revealing our age! We have always had a rhythm when it comes to storytelling and creating, but who would have thought all those years ago would lead to this? Honestly, this book is so much more because of you! I love your family—Zara, Sion and Beau Saulwick.

Sibella Court. Bell, honestly, I pinch myself that we are friends, you're so talented and so incredibly beautiful. Thank you for all the work you put into bringing your chapter to life. I appreciate all you have given me: life is better spent in a community of like-minded souls of which I count you among. Thank you.

Prestel Publishing, Holly La Due, and Claudia Stäuble. Thanks for all your help making this happen and for believing in my project and ideas. I feel so blessed to have such a great publisher and team of people backing my book and seeing it come to life.

Ariella Werner-Seidler. Thanks for just being such a talent. Honestly. I'm so grateful to you and to all that you have put into my brand and my world. I appreciate you and your big heart.

Rachel Carter. Thank you for always editing my work with such grace, fun and flair. Always with no judgment, you bring humor to my work. I appreciate your hard work and the love that you pour into what you do.

Sarah Frish. Thanks for translating my imagination into words. I appreciate you.

Mum, Dad and my brothers and sisters, thank you for raising me to love the outdoors, for never holding me back and for sparking my imagination and artistic inquisitiveness.

Thank you to all the parents and children that tasted the food, tested the recipes and allowed their faces to be featured throughout this book. The joy shown on the pages is truly a reflection of these amazing children and the outstanding job you parents have done raising them.

I am eternally grateful to Father God for every soul that helped with this book. It is my prayer that this book will inspire community and a connection between people of all ages and walks of life. It is my hope that we can come together and work towards leaving this world a better place than we found it and provide and give back to future generations. This book is my gift to you. Blessings upon blessings to you.

Thank you to all our *Wild Child* parents and kids:

Jordana Henry, Troy Wilkinson and Minty
David Child, Kat Parker and Jax
Holly McCauley, Nich Zalmstra, Della and Posey
Amelia Fullarton, Alan Rushforth, Arlo, Agnes and Ottie
Tash and Nathan Kelly, Sana and Taki
Courtney Adamo, Marlow, Easton and Ivy
Aimee Winchester, Clementine, Daisy, Autumn, Coco and Juni
Maddy Hadley, Zara, Sion and Beau Saulwick
Lotte Barnes and Ophelia
Justine and Nat Edwards, Saige
Casey and Marty Johnston, Ozzy and Raph
Maki Jahn, Malou and Mokky
Ellie Borenstein, Mason and Rocky
Carla Ellis, Yeera Laurie and Nyan Laurie
Jonas Widjaja, Luka and Arlo
Sibella Court, Silver
Yvonn Deitch, Matilda, Frida and Leon
Chelsea and Che Bagshaw and Cloudy
Ramas King
Sachin Smith

© Prestel Verlag, Munich · London · New York 2021
A member of Penguin Random House Verlagsgruppe GmbH
Neumarkter Strasse 28 · 81673 Munich

Library of Congress Control Number: 2020951904
A CIP catalogue record for this book is available from the British Library.

Editorial direction Prestel: Holly La Due, Claudia Stäuble
Copyediting: Lauren Salkeld
Recipe editor: Rachel Carter
Design and layout: Holly McCauley
Production management: Corinna Pickart
Separations: Reproline mediateam
Printing and binding: DZS Grafik d.o.o., Ljubljana

Penguin Random House Verlagsgruppe FSC® N001967

Printed in Slovenia

ISBN 978-3-7913-8720-8

www.prestel.com